KT-563-386

HOW TO BE A PERFECT PRANKSTER

- Choose the right target or audience.
  Pick people with a sense of humour.

- Choose the right time and place.
  For example, don't do pranks at school.

- Be responsible. Don't pull pranks that
  are dangerous, hurtful or destructive.

- After playing a prank, admit to being
  the prankster. Then be sure to clean up
  any messes made.

BISCUIT SURPRISE!

Serve up an unexpected sandwich biscuit! Play a savoury trick on your friends with some sandwich biscuits and hummus. Your friends will be in for a surprising dose of protein.

What You Need:

- 1 packet of sandwich biscuits
- butter knife
- hummus

CONTENTS

LIBRARIES NI
WITHDRAWN FROM STO

HOW TO PULL THE PERFECT PRANK

Do you get a good laugh from playing tricks on your friends? Who doesn't? If you're a prankster, these easy and funny gags are sure to keep your friends off balance.

What You Do:

1. Carefully pull apart the crème biscuits.

2. Use the butter knife to gently scrape off the crème filling.

3. Replace the crème filling with a layer of hummus.

4. Put the biscuits back together.

BOO! I CAN SEE YOU!

With a few simple supplies, you can play a trick on your entire family. Boo! The food in the fridge is staring back at you!

What You Need:

- googly eyes of different sizes
- scissors
- double-sided tape

What You Do:

1. Cut small circles of tape and attach to the back of the googly eyes.

2. Stick the googly eyes on various items in the refrigerator when no one is looking.

TIP! Get creative! Use some felt to add tongues, eyebrows or ears to your fridge friends.

UNDRINKABLE DRINKS

Your friends will be excited to gulp
down this delicious juice. Until they
realize it's undrinkable, that is! This
juice is actually gelatin, making it
impossible to slurp.

What You Need:

- 1 packet of red gelatin
- a measuring jug
- water
- whisk
- clear glasses
- drinking straws

What You Do:

1. Prepare the gelatin according to packet instructions.

2. Carefully pour the liquid gelatin into clear glasses.

3. Place a drinking straw into each glass.

4. Place the glasses in the fridge to allow the gelatin to set.

5. Surprise your friends with their undrinkable drinks!

CAUTION!

Ask an adult to help you when preparing the gelatin and using boiling water.

RAT PROBLEM

Rats - we have a rodent problem!
Freak out your friends with a beetroot
that looks like a huge rat. Be prepared
to cover your ears as they scream!

What You Need:

- a beetroot with a long
  root still attached
- sharp knife
- cereal or snack box

What You Do:

1. Cut off the bottom of the beetroot with the knife so it lays flat.

2. Place a cereal or snack box on its side. Then place the beetroot inside so the long root faces outwards.

TIP! Ask an adult to help when using the sharp knife.

EGGS-SCUSE ME!

Do you want to give someone a chuckle with breakfast? Give the eggs in your refrigerator a little personality.

What You Need:

- permanent marker pens
- a box of eggs

What You Do:

1. Use the pens to draw terrified faces on the eggs. You could include fake "cracks" in their heads.

2. Ask your parent or guardian if you can have eggs for breakfast. Watch them gasp and giggle when they open the egg box!

TIP! You could add a word bubble that reads, "Don't eat me!"

SPONGE BROWNIES

Imagine seeing a really tasty iced-chocolate brownie. You take a big bite and ... yuck! The brownie looks real, but it definitely doesn't taste it!

What You Need:

- scissors
- 1 dry kitchen sponge
- butter knife
- chocolate icing
- sprinkles (optional)

TIP! Make sure your target doesn't actually swallow any sponge!

What You Do:

1. Cut the sponge in half using the scissors.

2. Use the butter knife to spread chocolate icing all over the sponge squares. Make sure all sides are well-covered, except the bottoms.

3. Add some sprinkles, and wait for someone to take a bite!

TIP!

Be extra sneaky by including one or two "sponge brownies" on a plate of real brownies. Bad luck will decide who gets the spongy treats!

BUGS EVERYWHERE!

Give your friends a creepy surprise.
First get creative with creepy crawlies.
Then watch your friends jump in fear
when they turn on the lights!

What You Need:

- pencil
- bug or insect stencils
- black sugar paper
- scissors
- tape

What You Do:

1. Trace the shapes of insects and bugs onto the black paper.

2. Cut them out with the scissors.

3. Stick the fake bugs inside a lamp shade or ceiling light.

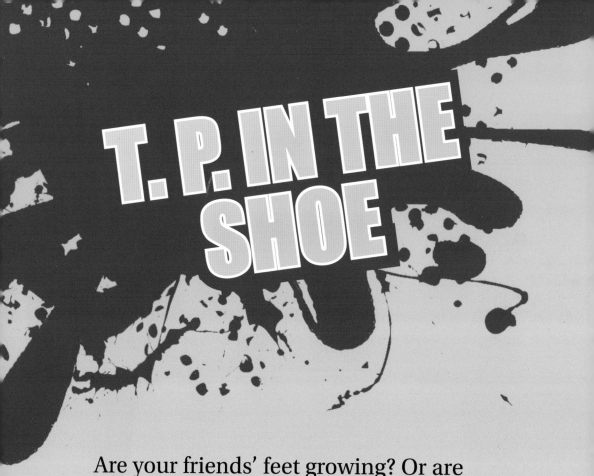

T. P. IN THE SHOE

Are your friends' feet growing? Or are their shoes shrinking? Pull this trick on all your friends and they'll think that their feet grew overnight!

What You Need:

- toilet paper or tissues
- several of your friends' shoes

What You Do:

1. Make sure your friends aren't near by.

2. Place balled up toilet paper or tissues inside the toes of their shoes. Make sure the tissue isn't visible.

3. Laugh and watch while they try to put their shoes on!

ICE CUBE CREATURES

Want to freak out your family at dinner time? This old but great prank is easy to do. And it's sure to scare the appetite out of your victims.

What You Need:
- ice cube tray
- water
- small plastic bugs or insects
- clear glasses
- water or juice

What You Do:

1. Fill an ice cube tray with water.

2. Slide the plastic bugs into each cube slot in the tray.

3. Place the tray in the freezer.

4. At dinner time offer to pour the drinks. Put a couple of ice cubes into each glass. Then add water or juice.

5. Get ready to watch your family and friends squirm!

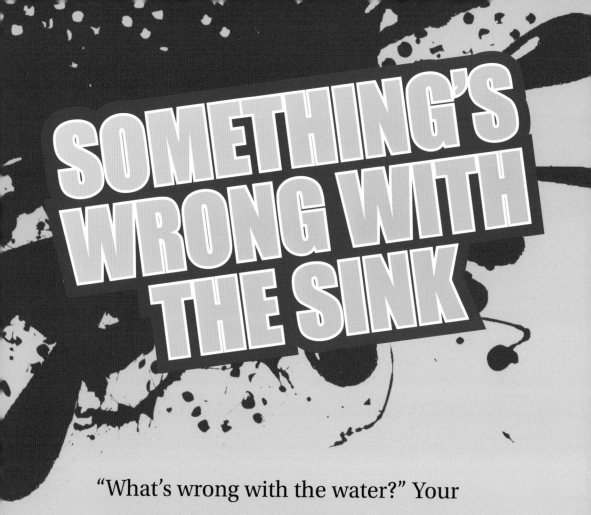

SOMETHING'S WRONG WITH THE SINK

"What's wrong with the water?" Your friends will get a shock when crazy coloured water pours from the tap. The colour lasts only a few seconds, but this trick will leave everyone laughing!

What You Need:

- cotton bud
- non-toxic, gel food colouring

What You Do:

1. Use the cotton bud to smear gel food colouring inside the tap.

2. Ask your friend to turn the water on to get you a glass of water.

EARLY WAKE-UP CALL

Looking for a simple trick to play on someone? Use this one to give your friend an extra-early wake-up call! However - you may want to sleep on the opposite side of the house!

What You Need:

- radio alarm clock

What You Do:

1. Make sure your victim has an alarm clock. When he or she isn't in the room, work out how to set the alarm.

2. Set the alarm for early in the morning, such as 4.00 am. Turn the volume up extra loud.

3. Sit back and relax while he or she wakes up too early. Warning: your friend might be really grumpy that day!

FIND OUT MORE

BOOKS

Dick and Dom's Whoopee Book of Practical Jokes, Richard McCourt and Dominic Wood (Macmillan Children's Books, 2015)

The Twits, Roald Dahl (Puffin, 2017)

WEBSITES

www.activityvillage.co.uk/animal-jokes
Activity Village

www.bbc.co.uk/cbbc/quizzes/bp-finish-the-joke-quiz
BBC

https://learnenglishkids.britishcouncil.org/en/jokes
British Council